The Forest Giants

A Malaysian folk tale

retold by **Rosalind Kerven**
Illustrated by **Georgie Birkett**

OXFORD
UNIVERSITY PRESS

Once upon a time, there was a thick green forest.

Lots of people lived in the forest.
Lots of giants lived in the forest too!

The giants were very wicked.
They liked to turn people into trees.

"How can we get rid of these giants?" said the people.
"Let's play a trick on them," said a woman.

"Let's make them think that we are bigger and stronger than them."

On the next day they made a very big cradle. An old man got in it.

The old man had no hair and no teeth.
He looked just like a big baby.

Soon the giants came along.
They looked inside the cradle.
"What a big baby!" shouted the giants.

"It will be much bigger than us when it grows up," they said.
The giants were scared of the baby and they ran away.

The old man told his friends.
"Let's play another trick on them,"
he said.

The people got a rake.
They twisted some long grass in it.
Then a girl hid behind a tree.

Soon the giants came along again.
They saw the rake.
"What's this?" shouted the giants.

"Don't touch that!" shouted the girl.
"It's my comb!"

"What a big comb!" shouted the giants.
"Look at these long hairs!"

The giants were scared and they ran away.

The girl told her friends.
"Let's play another trick on them," she said.

Some men climbed up a tall tree and cut off some branches.

Soon the giants came along again.
They saw the tree.

"Look at that tree!" shouted the giants.
"How did the people cut off
the branches?
They must be much bigger than us."

The giants thought that they were little and the people were big!

They were very scared.

The giants were so scared they packed their bags and ran right away.